MORE
FROZEN
DRINKS

WITH
OR
WITHOUT
THE
BUZZ

BY BRUCE WEINSTEIN

MORE FROZEN DRINKS

WITH OR WITHOUT THE BUZZ

Clarkson Potter/Publishers
New York

To my mom, who willingly
gave me the kitchen before I even
knew what to do with it.

●

Published by Clarkson Potter/Publishers, New York, New York.
Member of the Crown Publishing Group..

Random House, Inc.
New York, Toronto, London, Sydney, Auckland

www.randomhouse.com

CLARKSON N. POTTER is a trademark and
POTTER and colophon are registered
trademarks of Random House, Inc.

Previously published in different form as Frozen Drinks
by Clarkson Potter/Publishers in 1997.

DESIGN BY LISA GOLDENBERG

ISBN 0-676-79392-4

10 9 8 7 6 5 4 3 2 1
SECOND EDITION

ACKNOWLEDGMENTS

Heartfelt thanks to my dear friends Howard Rosner and Carl Ray for graciously turning over their house and blender; to my sister, Julie, for endlessly tasting drinks; to my friend and colleague Jody Weatherstone for helping to start this project in the first place; to my editor, Katie Workman, for making it all seem so easy; and to Mark for his constant encouragement and pride.

TABLE OF CONTENTS

INTRODUCTION

A scorching summer afternoon used to bring refreshing thoughts of paper cones dripping with melting shaved ice saturated with sweet, sticky syrups in bright fluorescent colors. Today, when the mercury climbs, you blow up the floating giraffe, check the pH balance in the pool, invite a few friends over, and plug in the blender. With only a few simple berries, ice cream, coffee, and a rainbow of juices and nectars, you can transport yourself and your friends to a place where central air conditioning is nothing more than a balmy breeze blowing off an azure sea.

YOUR BLENDER is the most important tool in your kitchen when it comes to making great drinks. Look for one with multiple speeds and sharp blades. Some come with glass pitchers, some with stainless steel. With glass, you can see what's happening inside the pitcher, but most bars use stainless-steel pitchers, because they don't break when you drop them. Glass blenders are easier to clean, with removable bottoms and replaceable blades. Most stainless-steel blenders don't have removable bottoms, so when the blades get dull and your drinks don't blend well, you will need to replace the whole metal pitcher. Don't worry, though—this can take years and hundreds of pounds of ice. As for cleaning, a simple rinse between drinks is sufficient whether you use metal or glass, but a good washing is important when you're finished for the day.

ICE is one of the few things that every frozen drink has in common. How hard your ice cubes are will affect the texture of your frozen drink. Ice that comes out of a very cold freezer is tough on your blender and may leave chunks of unblended ice in your drink. For a creamier, smoother drink, let your ice sit at room temperature for 10 to 15 minutes before blending. If it is very hot outside or if you don't have air conditioning, keep the ice in the refrigerator for half an hour before using. Just remember to drain any excess water before measuring the ice for your drinks. Once it has softened, the ice will blend smoothly and easily. Also, the smaller the ice cubes, the easier they will blend into smooth, creamy drinks. So if you have an automatic ice maker in your freezer with an adjustable setting, set it to make the smallest cubes possible. If you make your own ice cubes with trays, fill the trays only halfway. If necessary, you can always place larger ice cubes in a resealable bag and lightly pound them with the bottom of a heavy pot to break up the ice. Remember, you don't need to crush the ice into snow, just break it into small pieces that your blender can handle. If your refrigerator dispenses crushed ice, go ahead and use it.

FRESH FRUITS are the center of many of the drink recipes in this book. Choosing the right fruit will make the difference between an inferior frozen drink and a delicious one. Except for bananas, fruits should look fresh and unblemished. Peaches, apricots, melons, and pineapples should have a wonderful sweet aroma, even before you cut them open. Chances are, if a fruit has no smell before you cut it, it will have no taste when it is peeled and sliced. Note that kiwis with no aroma can still be sweet and juicy inside. Most fruits, including kiwis, should be firm but not hard. They should give slightly when you press them but not so much that your finger goes through the skin. Bananas are the only fruit that should be on the verge of rotting. The riper they are, the sweeter they are. Using underripe bananas that still have a green tint to them will give your drinks a slightly bitter taste. The berries you choose should be plump, sweet-smelling, and free of mold. Do not wash berries until you are ready to use them, and then give them only a gentle rinse.

CANNED AND FROZEN FRUIT can be used some of the time, when fresh fruits are unavailable. Canned apricots, drained out of heavy syrup, are full of flavor. Even canned orange and grapefruit sections make a good substitution for fresh. However, canned peaches lack an intense flavor and do not work as a substitution. If you have your heart set on a peach drink in the middle of winter, defrost some frozen peaches and taste them before using— sometimes frozen peaches taste wonderful and other times they have no flavor at all.

One solution is to freeze your own sliced peaches and berries during the summer so you can have juicy, sweet fruits for drinks all winter long. To freeze berries, simply spread them out on a tray in one layer and freeze until hard, then transfer to a container or resealable bag and store in the freezer. When berries defrost, they lose their shape and volume, so measure them while they are frozen and still have their natural shape. In general, when using frozen fruits, follow the recipe instructions exactly so that you know when to use them while they are still frozen and when to wait until they have thawed. Using frozen fruits while they are still frozen sometimes makes a drink too thick to blend.

FRUIT NECTARS come in a number of different brands and are readily available in most supermarkets. Libby's tend to be the most intense in flavor and have a thick consistency, while Goya nectars are sweeter and thinner. Try a few brands until you find your favorite. Also check the baby-food aisle—tropical fruit baby food makes a wonderful substitution for fruit nectars. Simply add 1 or 2 tablespoons of apple juice to thin them out until the baby food has the consistency of a runny puree. You may also need to add a teaspoon of sugar to help heighten the flavor.

FRUIT AND NUT SYRUPS are often found in the supermarket, near the ice cream toppings or chocolate sauces. They're becoming quite popular in coffee bars as flavor additions to coffee and cappuccino. Many coffeehouses also sell flavored syrups. Almond and tamarind syrups are often available in Italian markets. You can also buy syrups and nectars through the mail, from mail-order businesses or store catalogs. Check the resource guide at the back of this book for a listing.

ICE CREAM AND SHERBET need to be softened to blend smoothly, just as ice cubes do. Simply let the ice cream or sherbet sit at room temperature for 15 to 20 minutes before using, or give it a quick 10 seconds in the microwave, being careful not to melt it completely (unless, of course, the recipe calls for melted ice cream).

SWEETENERS come in all colors, flavors, and textures, but most of the recipes in this book call for superfine sugar. Also called instant dissolving sugar or bar sugar, it is available in your supermarket in one-pound easy-pour boxes. Some bartending books call for a simple syrup, which is sugar and water boiled together, but I prefer the superfine sugar because it is readily available and so much easier. If for some reason you cannot find superfine sugar, a good substitute is light corn syrup. Just use the same amount that the recipe calls for in superfine sugar.

If you prefer to make your own simple syrup, add 4 cups water to 4 cups sugar and boil together for 5 minutes in a large saucepan. Let the solution cool, then store it in a bottle in the refrigerator. When following a recipe, use $1\frac{1}{2}$ times the amount of simple syrup as you would sugar.

Honey is another sweetener that works well in frozen drinks, but it adds a very distinctive, strong flavor that doesn't always work well with the delicate flavors of tropical fruits and juices. In general, don't use honey unless the recipe calls for it.

Unfortunately, artificial sweeteners don't have the body or texture for creamy frozen drinks. With the amount of natural sugar that is present in fruits, juices, nectars, and flavored syrups, substituting aspartame or saccharin for 1 teaspoon sugar is not going to make a big difference anyway.

MIXERS can also be found in the supermarket, usually near the beer aisle. Sour mixer, collins mixer, and margarita mixer all have similar flavors, but margarita mixer has a hint of orange, while the other two have a lemon-lime flavor. Angostura makes a sweetened lime juice that I find has a fresher taste than the other brands, although there are many choices. Sweetened cream of coconut also comes in many brands, all of which are acceptable. Unsweetened coconut milk can be found in the Asian foods aisle and is now available in reduced-fat formulas. It is not as rich or as intensely flavored as regular coconut milk, but if you're watching your fat intake, it's a good option to have.

GARNISHING frozen drinks can be as much fun as making and drinking them, so be creative. Use fresh fruits with contrasting colors, chopped nuts, whipped cream, crumbled cookies, and candy bars. When using fruits like apples and pears—which turn brown when sliced and exposed to air—dip the slices into a solution of equal parts water and lemon juice before garnishing your drinks. Long straws are a must for tall frozen drinks, and plastic monkeys and paper umbrellas are worth seeking out. Frozen drinks look even more refreshing when you serve them in frosted glasses. To frost a glass, place it in the freezer for 10 minutes before you need it. When you remove it, moisture in the air will condense on the outside of the glass, creating a frosted look.

COCKTAIL VERSIONS with alcohol have been added to many recipes in this book. Note that almost every cocktail version requires more ice to compensate for the added liquid, so make sure you have plenty on hand before you begin.

It is important to be careful when drinking alcoholic beverages in the sun. The sun can cause dehydration, and alcohol can intensify this effect, so remember to drink plenty of water with your frozen cocktails, and exercise moderation.

1 SIMPLE FRUIT AND FLAVORED DRINKS

SPICED SEA BREEZE SLUSH

This drink is a slushy version of that classic summer refresher, the Sea Breeze—but with a twist. Fruit juice concentrates keep the drink spicy and tart, making it perfect for the dog days of summer or a slow afternoon in the depths of December. It's so thick, you'll want to serve it with spoons, not straws.

> ½ CUP CRANBERRY JUICE CONCENTRATE, THAWED
> ½ CUP ORANGE JUICE CONCENTRATE, THAWED
> ½ CUP WATER
> ½ TEASPOON VANILLA EXTRACT
> ¼ TEASPOON GROUND CINNAMON
> 2 CUPS ICE
> 2 ORANGE WEDGES, FOR GARNISH (OPTIONAL)

Combine the cranberry juice concentrate, orange juice concentrate, water, vanilla, cinnamon, and ice in a blender. Pulse the blender four or five times, until the mixture is well-combined. You may need to scrape down the blender's sides, then blend the drink until it is thick and slushy.

Pour into two glasses. Garnish with orange wedges, if desired.

■ Makes two 10-ounce drinks

Cocktail Versions

To make this frozen concoction a cocktail classic, add ¼ cup plain vodka to the blender before pulsing it. To put a new twist on things, you may want to try ¼ cup orange vodka, currant vodka, or cinnamon vodka before pulsing. Whichever vodka you choose, add 2 extra ice cubes to keep the drink slushy.

FROZEN PEACH SUNSET

This drink is very picturesque, with tiny flecks of pink and shocking streaks of red shooting up from the bottom of the creamy yellow blend. Make an extra one of these just to look at while you drink the other.

1½ CUPS ICE
¾ CUP PEACH NECTAR
1 WHOLE PEACH, PITTED AND SLICED, UNPEELED
1 TABLESPOON BOTTLED SWEETENED LIME JUICE
2 TABLESPOONS NONALCOHOLIC GRENADINE SYRUP
FRESH MINT SPRIGS OR LIME WEDGES, FOR GARNISH
    (OPTIONAL)

Combine the ice, peach nectar, peach slices, and sweetened lime juice in the blender. Blend until smooth.

Pour 1 tablespoon grenadine syrup into the bottom of each of two 12-ounce glasses. Pour the frozen peach mixture on top of the grenadine. The syrup should partially mix, sending brilliant red streaks up to the top of the glass. Garnish with a sprig of fresh mint or a wedge of lime, if desired.

■ Makes two 12-ounce drinks

Cocktail Versions

Add 3 ounces white rum and 1 ounce Southern Comfort before blending. Add an extra ice cube or two to keep the drink thick and slushy.

If apricots were used, try adding 3 ounces golden rum and 1 ounce apricot brandy, along with the extra ice cube(s).

Variation

FROZEN APRICOT SUNSET
Replace the peach nectar with apricot nectar. Replace the peach with two pitted sliced apricots (fresh or canned), unpeeled.

FROZEN RASPBERRY LEMONADE

The tartness of juicy raspberries marries well with the natural tang of lemon in this simple combination, which could easily become your summer favorite.

1 (10-OUNCE) PACKAGE FROZEN RASPBERRIES IN SYRUP
(SEE NOTE), THAWED
2 CUPS ICE
1/2 CUP LEMONADE CONCENTRATE, THAWED
1/2 CUP ICE WATER
RASPBERRIES AND MINT SPRIGS, FOR GARNISH (OPTIONAL)

Measure 3/4 cup of the raspberries with some syrup and pour into a blender. Refrigerate the remaining berries and syrup for another time. Add the ice, lemonade concentrate, and ice water to the blender. Pulse the blender until the mixture blends easily. Then continue to blend on high until the mixture is completely smooth and free of any ice chunks.

Pour into two glasses and garnish with fresh raspberries and a mint sprig, if desired.

■ Makes two 12-ounce drinks

NOTE: If you don't like raspberry seeds, press the thawed soft berries (and syrup) through a sieve before adding to the blender.

Variation

FROZEN CHERRY LEMONADE
Use 3/4 cup fresh cherries or drained canned sweet pitted cherries, instead of raspberries.

Cocktail Versions

Replace half the ice water with vodka. Reduce the frozen berries and syrup by 1/4 cup and add 1/4 of any raspberry-flavored liqueur, such as framboise. Also, add an extra ice cube or two.

If using cherries, try 1/4 cup cherry liqueur instead of framboise.

APPLE BERRY BRAIN BLASTER

Similar to the so-called brain drinks you get at national juice chains, this chilly concoction is the perfect pick-me-up for the middle of a long day. The berries are loaded with essential vitamins—and the applesauce has the carbs you'll need to get going again. You might also want to serve this sweet drink before lunch as an appetizing starter, or after dinner as a luscious dessert.

1/2 CUP APPLESAUCE
1/3 CUP FROZEN RASPBERRIES
1/3 CUP FROZEN BLACKBERRIES
4 LARGE FRESH STRAWBERRIES, HULLED AND HALVED
3/4 CUP APPLE JUICE
1 1/2 CUPS ICE
2 LARGE STRAWBERRIES, FOR GARNISH (OPTIONAL)

Combine the applesauce, raspberries, blackberries, strawberries, apple juice, and ice in a blender. Pulse the blender six or seven times, until the mixture is thick and smooth.

Pour into two glasses. Garnish each glass with a whole strawberry on the rim, if desired.

■ Makes two 12-ounce drinks

Cocktail Versions

Apples and rum are a perfect combination. Simply add 1/4 cup gold rum to the blender before pulsing. Fruit-flavored liqueurs like apple schnapps and crème de framboise (or Chambord) can give this drink a real kick (add 1 ounce of either). Add 2 extra ice cubes to keep the drink icy.

PEACH APRICOT FROZEN TEA

In the South, everyone enjoys an enormous glass of plain iced tea with a meal or all on its own. But if Southerners knew about this peach apricot concoction, they might reconsider their options. Try this fruity, frozen beverage any time of day, from early morning to late at night.

> 1 PEACH
> 2 TABLESPOONS SWEETENED INSTANT ICED TEA MIX
> ½ CUP APRICOT NECTAR
> JUICE OF ½ LEMON (ABOUT 2 TABLESPOONS)
> 1½ CUPS ICE

Cut the peach in half. Remove the pit and discard it. Slice the peach and place it into a blender. Add the instant tea mix, apricot nectar, lemon juice, and ice. Pulse the machine once or twice to get the drink blended, then blend it until the mixture is smooth.

Pour into two glasses.

> ■ Makes two 10-ounce drinks

Cocktail Versions

Bourbon can makes this iced tea a very Southern drink. Add 3 ounces bourbon and 1½ ounces peach schnapps before blending. Or simply add ¼ cup Southern Comfort before blending. Also, add 2 or 3 extra ice cubes to keep the drink smooth.

RASPBERRY ALMOND FROST

This cold combination of raspberries and almonds may remind you of the classic linzertorte, but it's just a little lighter and a lot more refreshing.

> ½ CUP FRESH OR FROZEN RASPBERRIES
>   IN SYRUP (SEE NOTE)
> 2 CUPS ICE
> 1 CUP CRAN-RASPBERRY JUICE
> ⅓ CUP ALMOND SYRUP
> WHOLE ROASTED ALMONDS AND MINT SPRIGS, FOR
>   GARNISH (OPTIONAL)

If using frozen raspberries, measure them frozen, but let them defrost before blending. Combine the berries, ice, Cran-Raspberry juice, and almond syrup in the blender. Pulse the blender until the mixture blends easily, then continue to blend on high until the drink is completely smooth.

Pour into two glasses and garnish with whole roasted almonds and a mint sprig, if desired.

■ Makes two 12-ounce drinks

NOTE: If you don't like raspberry seeds, press the thawed soft berries (and syrup) through a sieve before adding to the blender.

Cocktail Version

Both vodka and white rum will work nicely in this drink. Add 3 ounces of either before blending. Also, add an extra ice cube or two to keep the drink thick and slushy.

PINK GRAPEFRUIT FREEZE

Even people who don't normally like grapefruit keep asking for this Slurpee-like drink. That's because the grenadine syrup mellows out the tart edge of the grapefruit and makes this summer cooler smooth, sweet, and delicious.

1 CUP ICE
1/3 CUP GRAPEFRUIT JUICE CONCENTRATE, THAWED
2/3 CUP WATER
1/4 CUP NONALCOHOLIC GRENADINE SYRUP
1 TO 3 TEASPOONS SUPERFINE SUGAR (OPTIONAL)
FRESH MINT SPRIGS, FOR GARNISH (OPTIONAL)

Combine the ice, grapefruit juice concentrate, water, and grenadine syrup in the blender. Pulse it until the mixture is thick and slushy. Taste the mixture with a spoon. If you want it sweeter, add the superfine sugar one teaspoon at a time, stopping the blender and tasting again after each addition.

Pour into two glasses and garnish with mint sprigs, if desired.

■ Makes two 10-ounce drinks

Cocktail Versions

Replace the grenadine syrup with Campari.

Or replace half the grenadine syrup with Campari and add 2 ounces vodka before blending. You will also need to add an extra ice cube or two to keep the drink thick and slushy.

SOUR LEMON SIPPER

Served in a tall glass with a long spoon, this drink will make any afternoon pass slowly, quietly, and deliciously. The world will just fade away. Instead of plain lemonade, try serving this frozen slush to your houseguests. But be forewarned—they will definitely linger in your home!

1½ CUPS LEMON SORBET
½ CUP LEMONADE
½ CUP GINGER ALE
2 LEMON SLICES, FOR GARNISH (OPTIONAL)

Combine the lemon sorbet, lemonade, and ginger ale in the blender. Blend the drink only until it is just combined, in three or four quick pulses—you want to keep as much of the fizz as you can.

Pour into two glasses. Garnish each glass with a lemon slice, if desired.

■ Makes two 8-ounce drinks

Cocktail Versions

For an even slower afternoon, add 3 ounces plain vodka before blending. You might also add ½ ounce lemon liqueur to the mix. Or simply add 3 ounces lemon-flavored vodka before blending. In any case, increase the lemon sorbet to 1¾ cups to keep the drink thick and slushy.

ORCHARD
BLUES

Blueberries are naturally rich and full of pectin, so they make this drink thick and satisfying. The nectarines combine with the berries to turn the drink a beautiful mauve. It will be tinged with flecks of deep purple—as tantalizing as it is appetizing.

> 1 NECTARINE
> 1/2 CUP FRESH BLUEBERRIES
> 1/2 CUP ORANGE JUICE
> 2 TABLESPOONS ALMOND SYRUP (ALSO CALLED "ORGEAT,"
>   OR "ORZATA"—SEE NOTE)
> 2 CUPS ICE
> 2 MINT SPRIGS, FOR GARNISH (OPTIONAL)

Cut the nectarine in half. Remove the pit and discard it. Slice the nectarine into a blender. Add the blueberries, orange juice, almond syrup, and ice. Blend until the drink is smooth and very thick, about 30 seconds.

Pour into two glasses. Garnish with mint sprigs, if desired.

> ■ Makes two 10-ounce drinks

NOTE: Almond syrup (or "orgeat," or "orzata") is a thick, sweet, concentrated syrup, often available at gourmet markets and specialty stores. It is not to be confused with almond extract, an alcohol-based flavoring.

Cocktail Versions

To make a light cocktail, omit the almond syrup and add 2 tablespoons amaretto before blending. For a more potent drink, you can also add 3 ounces of white rum. Add 2 ice cubes as well, to keep the drink slushy.

RED ZINGER STINGER

With a touch of honey, this frozen tea is truly light and not too sweet. If you normally use artificial sweeteners in your iced tea, you might want to make an exception in this case. Sugarless sweeteners don't create a smooth slush in blended frozen drinks.

>   4 RED ZINGER TEA BAGS
>   2 CUPS BOILING WATER
>   3 TABLESPOONS HONEY (SEE PAGE 13)

Place the tea bags in the boiling water and let steep until cool. Pour 1¼ cups of the cool tea into ice cube trays and freeze. Combine the frozen cubes, remaining cold tea, and honey in a blender. Blend until slushy.

Pour into two glasses.

■ **Makes two 10-ounce drinks**

Variations

White sugar, brown sugar, and corn syrup also work well, and each adds its own flavor. Don't be afraid to experiment with your favorite teas and different kinds of sweeteners. Simply brew your favorite tea with twice as many tea bags as you normally would for hot tea. Lemon teas, spiced teas, and fruit-flavor teas taste the best. If you like baked apples, try this drink using apple spice tea bags with maple syrup.

MAPLE
TREE

It takes 30 to 50 gallons of maple sap for every gallon of pure maple syrup, which can make it an expensive treat. But a little goes a long way, so for this drink, splurge on the real thing. Regular pancake syrup just won't cut it.

1 CUP ICE
1/3 CUP APPLE JUICE
2 TABLESPOONS PURE MAPLE SYRUP (SEE NOTE)
JUICE OF 1/2 SMALL LIME (ABOUT 1 TABLESPOON)
1/4 TEASPOON VANILLA EXTRACT
FRESH APPLE RINGS, FOR GARNISH (OPTIONAL)
   (SEE PAGE 14)

Put the ice into a blender. Add the apple juice, maple syrup, lime juice, and vanilla. Pulse the blender a few times. The mixture will be thick, so you may need to stop the blender and scrape down the sides to get things moving. If the mixture is too thick to blend easily, add more apple juice, 1 tablespoon at a time, until the mixture blends smoothly. Continue to blend for about 20 seconds or until the mixture is smooth and free of any chunks of ice.

Pour into a glass and garnish with apple rings, if desired.

■ Makes one 10-ounce drink

NOTE: Pure maple syrup comes in different grades: light amber, medium amber, and dark amber. The lighter the syrup, the more delicate the flavor. When cooking with maple syrup, choose medium or dark amber so the flavor will carry through all the other ingredients.

Cocktail Version

Add 1 ounce dark rum and 1/2 ounce brandy before blending. If you can find Calvados (apple brandy), use that instead of the brandy. Also, add an extra ice cube or two to keep the drink thick and slushy.

CHERRY VANILLA SMOOTHIE

Tart, mildly sweet, this drink is kind of like an old-fashioned Cherry Lime Ricky, that drugstore favorite from years gone by. Use only frozen sweet cherries, or else the drink will be far too sour. And don't confuse vanilla syrup with vanilla extract—vanilla syrup is sweet and thick. It's usually found in the soft drink aisle or coffee section of most supermarkets.

> 1 CUP FROZEN SWEET CHERRIES
> 1/2 CUP WATER
> 1/4 CUP FRESH LIME JUICE
> 2 TABLESPOONS VANILLA SYRUP
> 1 TABLESPOON SUPERFINE SUGAR
> 1 CUP ICE

Combine the sweet cherries, water, lime juice, vanilla syrup, superfine sugar, and ice in a blender. Pulse three or four times until the drink is smooth. Then blend until the drink is thick, about 30 seconds. Since this drink is so thick, you may have to shake the blender once or twice to make sure everything is getting blended.

Pour into two glasses.

■ **Makes two 8-ounce drinks**

Cocktail Versions

Cherries and vodka are perfect together. It's too bad no vodka company has thought of it. But if you add 3 ounces plain vodka to the drink before blending, you'll beat them to the punch. Add 2 or 3 extra ice cubes, so the drink will stay slushy.

2

MELON AND TROPICAL FRUIT DRINKS

ARCTIC WATERMELON ICE

To make this drink, you will need to first prepare some watermelon juice. Make a lot—it's simple and will stay fresh in the refrigerator for a week. Watermelon juice also makes great ice pops. Just pour it into plastic ice-pop molds and freeze—they'll last for weeks in the freezer.

> 1 CUP ICE
> 1 CUP WATERMELON JUICE (RECIPE FOLLOWS)
> 1 TABLESPOON BOTTLED SWEETENED
>   LIME JUICE
> 1 TABLESPOON NONALCOHOLIC
>   GRENADINE SYRUP

Put the ice in a blender. Pour in the watermelon juice, sweetened lime juice, and grenadine. Blend until slushy and smooth.

Pour into a glass.

■ **Makes one 12-ounce drink**

WATERMELON JUICE

> 1 (2–3 POUND) WEDGE OF WATERMELON
> 1/2 CUP CORN SYRUP

Cut the rind off the watermelon. Remove as many seeds as you can and roughly chop the melon. You will need 3 cups. Put the melon and the corn syrup in a blender and blend until the mixture is liquefied. Pour through a strainer, discarding any foam and seeds that don't go through. If any foam passes through the strainer, simply skim it off. Pour the juice into a jar or pitcher, cover, and refrigerate until needed. The juice will stay fresh for about a week.

■ **Makes about 2 1/2 cups**

SWEET MANGO LASSI

Lassis are classic Indian yogurt drinks, perfumed with flowers and flavored with exotic fruits and sometimes even salt. Made with nonfat yogurt, the delicate essence of roses, and the subtle flavor of mango, this lassi is a surprisingly light and refreshing frozen drink.

1 SMALL MANGO
1 CUP NONFAT PLAIN YOGURT
1 CUP ICE
1 TABLESPOON HONEY
¼ TEASPOON ROSE WATER (SEE NOTE)

Peel the mango and cut the flesh away from the pit. Roughly chop the fruit. You will need ½ cup. Put the mango, yogurt, ice, honey, and rose water in a blender and blend until completely smooth. Don't worry about overblending this drink, as it should have no trace of ice chunks at all.

Pour into two glasses.

■ Makes two 10-ounce drinks

NOTE: Rose water and orange-flower water are available in many drugstores and gourmet markets. Also check the resource guide at the back of the book.

Variations

Orange-flower water (see Note) has a lovely, delicate aroma and can replace rose water for a slightly different taste.

Use low-fat or whole-milk yogurt for a richer, creamier drink.

Use ½ cup peeled, seeded, and chopped papaya, guava, cactus pear, or cherimoya instead of mango. If these fresh tropical fruits are unavailable, use ⅓ cup canned fruit nectar instead. Mango, guava, pear, apricot, and peach are especially delicious.

FUZZY MELON SNOWBALL

The flavor of honeydew melon is too delicate to blend with ice, so partially freeze the melon before you make this drink. The semifrozen pieces of melon will give your drink a slushy consistency without using ice. If you don't have time to freeze the melon, make the drink with unfrozen fruit and serve over crushed ice. It won't technically be a frozen drink, but it will still be incredibly delicious. If you overfreeze your melon or buy frozen melon that is very hard, partially defrost it before blending.

1 SMALL HONEYDEW MELON
1/2 CUP PEACH NECTAR
1 TABLESPOON ORANGE JUICE CONCENTRATE, THAWED
1 TABLESPOON FRESH LIME JUICE
2 TEASPOONS SUPERFINE SUGAR
SMALL WATERMELON WEDGES,
    FOR GARNISH (OPTIONAL)

Cut the melon open and scoop out the seeds. Remove the rind and cut the melon into small cubes (about 1/2-inch pieces). Measure 2 cups melon cubes and freeze them in a plastic container or resealable bag until they are partially frozen. The melon cubes should be firm and frosty but not rock-hard. Use the leftover melon for fruit salad or freeze it all (in 2-cup packages) for the second and third round of drinks.

When the melon cubes are partially frozen, put them in a blender with the peach nectar, orange juice concentrate, lime juice, and sugar. Pulse the blender only until the mixture

Cocktail Version

Add 1 1/2 ounces vodka and 1 ounce melon liqueur. Also, add an extra ice cube or two to keep the drink thick and slushy.

is a slushy liquid. Do not overblend or the drink will lose its frozen consistency.

Pour into two glasses and garnish, if desired, with wedges of fresh watermelon, rind and all.

■ **Makes two 8-ounce drinks**

POG

POGs—small decorated cardboard circles—are the Hula Hoops of the nineties. They are everywhere. Kids flip them, trade them, and collect them. But few kids know that the POG craze started in Hawaii, with caps from bottles of pineapple, orange, and guava juice blend.

$\frac{1}{2}$ CUP ORANGE SHERBET
$\frac{1}{2}$ CUP GUAVA NECTAR
$\frac{1}{4}$ CUP PINEAPPLE JUICE

Put the sherbet, guava nectar, and pineapple juice in a blender and blend together until smooth. Pour over crushed ice or very small cubes.

■ **Makes one 10-ounce drink**

Cocktail Version

To make a POG cocktail, just add 1$\frac{1}{2}$ ounces golden rum before blending. This is one POG we don't recommend you give to your kids. Also, add an extra ice cube or two to keep the drink thick and slushy.

KIWI KOOLER

The mild graininess of the pear nectar combines with the tiny seeds in the brilliant green kiwi and the sweet aroma of the vanilla syrup to create an experience for each of the senses.

> 1 LARGE RIPE KIWI
> ⅓ CUP PEAR NECTAR OR JUICE
> 2 TEASPOONS SUPERFINE SUGAR
> 1 TABLESPOON VANILLA SYRUP (SEE PAGE 12)
> 1 CUP ICE
> UNPEELED KIWI AND PEAR WEDGES,
>   FOR GARNISH (OPTIONAL)

Peel the kiwi and remove the hard nib from the stem end. Slice the kiwi thinly and put in a blender with the pear nectar, sugar, and vanilla syrup. Blend for a few seconds to liquefy the kiwi. Turn off the blender and add the ice. Pulse the blender until the mixture starts to blend easily. Continue blending on high until the mixture is thick, slushy, and smooth.

Pour into a glass and garnish with an unpeeled kiwi wedge and a pear slice, if desired (see Note).

■ **Makes one 10-ounce drink**

NOTE: To keep your pear slices fresh and white, dip them in a little lemon juice mixed with water first.

Cocktail Version

A splash of white wine stirred in at the very end makes this a truly sophisticated frozen drink. Try a sweet white wine like a sweet Riesling or Lillet blanc.

TRIPLE TROPICAL DELIGHT

These days, exotic fruit juices and nectars are everywhere. Frankly, they're a boon to the budding mixologist because they're easier to find than many tropical fruits, and many brands use 100 percent real juice. This Triple Tropical Delight uses one common tropical fruit and two exotic juices: passion fruit and papaya. You'll end up with a tall, fruity drink: refreshing, light, and thoroughly delightful.

1 LARGE MANGO
1/2 CUP PASSION FRUIT NECTAR
1/3 CUP PAPAYA NECTAR
1 TABLESPOON BOTTLED SWEETENED LIME JUICE
2 TEASPOONS NONALCOHOLIC GRENADINE SYRUP
2 CUPS ICE
TWO 8-INCH PIECES OF PEELED SUGAR CANE, FOR GARNISH (OPTIONAL)

Peel, dice, and pit the mango. You'll need 2/3 cup mango pieces—you can reserve any extra for another use, such as fruit salad. Put the mango pieces in a blender. Add the passion fruit nectar, papaya nectar, sweetened lime juice, grenadine syrup, and ice. Blend until smooth, about 1 minute.

Pour into two glasses. Use peeled sugar cane sections as swizzle sticks, if desired.

■ Makes two 10-ounce drinks

Cocktail Versions

To make a simple cocktail, you can add 1/4 cup gold rum before blending. For the taste of a frozen Mai Tai, add 3 ounces gold rum and 1 1/2 ounces amaretto before blending. But always add 1 or 2 extra ice cubes to keep these cocktail versions thick and slushy.

PAPAYAN HAWAIIAN SNOWSTORM

Fresh papayas are a treat, tropical and sweet. They used to be rare, before those from Haiti started showing up in our markets. You can use either the South Pacific or the Caribbean varieties—but always use ones that are very ripe, almost entirely yellow, even with a few brown spots.

> 1 SMALL, RIPE PAPAYA
> 1 CUP COCONUT SORBET
> 1/2 CUP PASSION FRUIT NECTAR
> 1/2 CUP WATER
> 1 CUP ICE
> 2 EDIBLE FLOWERS, SUCH AS NASTURTIUMS, FOR GARNISH (OPTIONAL) (SEE NOTE)

Cut the papaya in half. Scoop out the seeds and discard them. Scoop the flesh into the blender and discard the skin. Add the coconut sorbet, passion fruit nectar, water, and ice to the blender. Pulse the blender until the drink is thick and smooth.

Pour into two glasses. Garnish with an edible flower, if desired.

■ Makes two 10-ounce drinks

NOTE: Edible flowers are available in many supermarkets and gourmet stores, along with the fresh herbs. Never use flowers from your garden unless you are completely sure they're edible and you have not sprayed them with any pesticides.

Cocktail Version

You only need 1/4 cup white rum to transport you and your guests to Tahiti. And it's much cheaper than the plane tickets. To keep the drink thick and slushy, add a few ice cubes to the blender, too.

KIWI BANANA SMOOTHIE

This classic blender drink is the right burst of energy you need—before or after the gym, before or after work, before or after the kids come home.

1 KIWI
1 MEDIUM BANANA
1/2 CUP VANILLA-FLAVORED YOGURT
1 TABLESPOON HONEY
1 CUP ICE
TWO 2-INCH PEELED BANANA SLICES, FOR GARNISH
    (OPTIONAL)

Peel the kiwi and the banana. Cut them each into quarters and place them in a blender. Add the yogurt, honey, and ice. Blend until the drink is thick and smooth, about 1 minute.

Pour into two glasses. Garnish with the bananas, if desired.

■ Makes two 8-ounce drinks

Variations

For a pretty color and a tangier flavor, you might want to add 1/4 cup fresh berries (blueberries, raspberries, or blackberries) before blending. Don't be afraid to experiment with other flavored yogurts, too—like lemon, blueberry, or strawberry-banana. For a healthy touch, you might want to add a little ginseng or Saint-John's-wort extract, both available at your local health food store.

DOUBLE MELON FREEZE

Not only delicious, this drink is also beautiful. You make it in two layers, the pale summery colors of cantaloupe and honeydew melon floating in the glass. Serve the drinks quickly, before the layers have a chance to melt and combine.

1 SMALL CANTALOUPE
1 SMALL HONEYDEW
⅓ CUP PEACH NECTAR
2 TEASPOONS SUPERFINE SUGAR, DIVIDED
⅓ CUP LYCHEE NECTAR (OR WHITE GRAPE JUICE)
2 MINT SPRIGS, FOR GARNISH (OPTIONAL)

Cut both melons open and scoop out the seeds. Remove the rinds and cut the melons into small cubes (about ½-inch thick), keeping the two types separate. Measure 1½ cups melon cubes from each melon. Still keeping them separate, place the cubes in freezer-safe plastic bags and freeze them until they are icy and firm, but not rock solid, about 1 hour. Reserve the remaining melon cubes for another use, such as fruit salad—or freeze them in other bags for further rounds of drinks (just allow them to thaw slightly before blending).

Put the frozen cantaloupe, peach nectar, and 1 teaspoon superfine sugar into a blender. Pulse until the mixture is thick and slushy. Divide the mixture between two glasses.

Rinse out the blender. Put the frozen honeydew, lychee nectar, and the remaining teaspoon sugar in the blender. Pulse until the mixture is thick and slushy. Carefully layer the honeydew mixture on top of the cantaloupe mixture in each of the glasses.

Garnish the two glasses with mint sprigs, if desired.

■ Makes two 12-ounce drinks

SWEET-SOUR CHERRY LYCHEE SLUSH

Fresh lychees are something that very few Americans ever experience. If you live in a city with a large Asian community, you might find fresh lychees in the markets from early spring through summer. Peel off the thick brown or red papery shell to reveal juicy white, sweet flesh surrounding a large, hard brown nut. Luckily, canned lychees retain all the flavor of fresh ones, although their texture is a bit firmer and drier.

1 (20-OUNCE) CAN WHOLE LYCHEES IN SYRUP (SEE NOTE)
1½ CUPS ICE
3 TABLESPOONS SOUR CHERRY OR BLACK
    CHERRY SYRUP (SEE PAGE 12)

Drain the lychees, reserving the liquid. Add 12 lychees, ¾ cup of the reserved liquid, the ice, and the sour cherry syrup to the blender. Blend on high until smooth.

Pour into two glasses.

■ Makes two 10-ounce drinks

NOTE: Canned lychees are available in the Asian food section in many large supermarkets or in many Asian markets. They are often on the menu at Chinese restaurants. Ask for a few orders to go, but make sure to ask for plenty of syrup with the fruit.

Cocktail Version

Vodka lends itself quite well to both lychees and cherries. Add 3 ounces before blending. Also, add an extra ice cube or two to keep the drink thick and slushy.

MARGAR

DAIQUIRIS, ~ITAS, AND COLADAS

ICY
BLACKBERRY
DAIQUIRI

Almost black on the vine, these berries blend into a brilliant purple drink that's both tart and sweet. The addition of black currant syrup (also called cassis) gives the drink a richness of flavor that the berries alone don't have.

> 1 CUP ICE
> 1/3 CUP BLACKBERRIES
> 1/4 CUP APPLE JUICE
> 1 TABLESPOON BLACK CURRANT SYRUP
>   (SEE PAGE 12)
> 2 TEASPOONS SUPERFINE SUGAR
> JUICE OF 1 SMALL LIME (ABOUT 1 1/2
>   TO 2 TABLESPOONS)
> RASPBERRIES, BLACKBERRIES, AND ROUND
>   LIME SLICES, FOR GARNISH (OPTIONAL)

Combine the ice, blackberries, apple juice, black currant syrup, sugar, and lime juice in a blender. Blend until completely smooth.

Pour into a glass and garnish with a couple of fresh red raspberries and blackberries and a lime wheel, if desired.

■ Makes one 12-ounce drink

Cocktail Version

Before blending, add 2 ounces white rum. Replace the black currant syrup with 1 tablespoon crème de cassis liqueur. Also add an extra ice cube or two to keep the drink thick and slushy.

HONEYDEW MARGARITA

The delicate taste of honeydew is enhanced, not hidden, by the sour lime in a margarita. The drink itself gets most of its body from the frozen fruit itself, since there's no added ice. Buy a honeydew melon that smells sweet and luscious—that way, you know your drinks will be, too.

> 1 SMALL HONEYDEW MELON
> ½ CUP BOTTLED MARGARITA, COLLINS, OR SOUR MIXER
> 1 TABLESPOON ORANGE JUICE CONCENTRATE, THAWED
> 1 TABLESPOON BOTTLED SWEETENED LIME JUICE
> ¼ CUP KOSHER SALT, FOR GARNISH ON THE RIMS OF THE GLASSES (OPTIONAL)

Cut the honeydew melon open and scoop out the seeds. Remove the rind and cut the flesh into small cubes (about ½-inch thick). Measure 2 cups melon cubes, and place them in a freezer-safe plastic bag. Freeze them until they are icy and firm, but not rock solid, about 1 hour. Reserve the remaining melon cubes for another use, such as fruit salad—or freeze them in other bags for further rounds of drinks (just remember to thaw them slightly before blending).

Put the melon pieces, mixer, orange juice concentrate, and lime juice in a blender. Blend until the mixture is smooth and slushy.

If desired, pour the salt on a small plate, wet the tops of two glasses, and rub the glasses into the salt, shaking off any excess. Pour the honeydew mixture into the two glasses.

■ Makes two 10-ounce drinks

Cocktail Version

Add 3 ounces tequila and 1 ounce Triple Sec before blending. Add 2 or 3 ice cubes to keep the drink thick and slushy.

SOUTH BEACH DAIQUIRI

This daiquiri requires you to remove the sections of the citrus fruits and discard all the surrounding membranes and white pith. Save the leftover juice and orange sections for another round of drinks.

> 1 LARGE ORANGE
> 1 SMALL GRAPEFRUIT
> 2 LARGE TANGERINES
> JUICE OF 2 SMALL LIMES (ABOUT ¼ CUP)
> 2 TABLESPOONS SUPERFINE SUGAR
> 2 CUPS ICE

Cut ½ inch off both ends of the orange, so that the fruit sits flat. Then start cutting from top to bottom, peeling off the rind and the thin membrane beneath. Cut between the sections, letting the sections drop into the bowl with the juice.

Measure out ½ cup orange segments and put in the blender. Save the remaining segments and juice for another time. Repeat this process with the grapefruit, measuring out ¼ cup segments and adding them to the blender. Repeat the process a third time with the tangerines, measuring out ½ cup segments and adding them to the blender. Add the lime juice, sugar, and ice to the fruit in the blender and blend on high until the mixture is smooth and slushy.

Pour into two glasses.

■ Makes two 12-ounce drinks

Cocktail Versions

Vodka is a natural with citrus fruits. Add 3 ounces before blending. For a more exotic flavor, also add ½ ounce Galliano, an Italian liqueur with a slight licorice flavor. Also, add an extra ice cube.

MOCK LIME DAIQUIRI

Ask for a daiquiri at any bar and you will get a drink that blends the wonderful tartness of limes with the sweetness of rum and sugar. This recipe uses a combination of different lime flavors to create a drink with a little more depth and character, even without the addition of rum (although that's still an option).

> 1½ CUPS ICE
> 2 TABLESPOONS FROZEN LIMEADE CONCENTRATE, THAWED
> 1 CUP LEMON-LIME GATORADE
> 1 TABLESPOON BOTTLED SWEETENED LIME JUICE
> ROUND LIME SLICES, FOR GARNISH (OPTIONAL)

Put the ice in a blender. Add the limeade concentrate, Gatorade, and lime juice. Blend on high until the mixture is completely smooth.

Pour into two glasses and garnish with lime wheels, if desired.

■ Makes two 8-ounce drinks

Cocktail Version

To create a daiquiri cocktail, blend 1½ ounces rum, 1 tablespoon fresh lime juice, and 2 teaspoons superfine sugar with 1 cup ice.

SMOOTH BANANA DAIQUIRI

The secret of this drink is in the banana, so use the ripest one you can find. Brown spots on the outside of the skin don't always mean brown spots on the inside. What you usually get is a soft, sweet, creamy banana that will give your frozen drinks an unforgettable flavor. The addition of banana syrup is optional, and will only heighten the effect.

1 LARGE VERY RIPE BANANA
1 CUP ICE
¼ CUP APPLE JUICE OR WHITE GRAPE JUICE
1 TABLESPOON BANANA SYRUP (SEE PAGE 12)
1 TEASPOON SUPERFINE SUGAR
JUICE OF 1 MEDIUM LIME (ABOUT 2 TABLESPOONS)
BANANA STICKS, FOR GARNISH (OPTIONAL) (SEE NOTE)

Peel the banana and break it into small pieces. Put the banana pieces in the blender with the ice, apple juice, banana syrup, sugar, and lime juice. Blend until completely smooth.

Pour into a glass and garnish with long banana sticks, if desired.

■ Makes one 12-ounce drink

NOTE: To make banana sticks, peel a long banana, slice it into four pieces lengthwise, then freeze until hard. Long banana sticks are a fun garnish for lots of drinks. You can even dip them in chocolate before freezing them for a garnish that's as decadent as it is delicious.

Cocktail Version

Before blending, add 2 ounces white rum. Replace the banana syrup with 2 tablespoons banana liqueur. Also, add an extra ice cube or two to keep the drink thick and slushy.

CALIFORNIA COLADA

Peaches are one of California's top crops—and combined with coconut, they twist this colada away from the run-of-the-mill and into something special. This drink has got a sunny, citrus taste—a refreshing summery feeling, even in the winter.

1/2 CUP PEACH NECTAR
1/4 CUP ORANGE JUICE CONCENTRATE, THAWED
2 TABLESPOONS CREAM OF COCONUT (SEE PAGE 52)
2 CUPS ICE
2 ORANGE WHEELS, FOR GARNISH (OPTIONAL)

Combine the peach nectar, orange juice concentrate, cream of coconut, and ice in a blender. Pulse until the drink is thick and smooth. You may need to stop the blender, scrape down the sides, and shake it once or twice to get the mixture thoroughly blended.

Pour into two glasses. Garnish with orange wheels, if desired.

■ Makes two 8-ounce drinks

Cocktail Versions

Add 3 ounces white rum before blending. For a jazzier cocktail, you might want to try 3 ounces spiced rum instead. Or use coconut rum for extra coconut flavor. In any event, add 1 or 2 extra ice cubes to keep the drink thick and slushy.

CHERRY PIE DAIQUIRI

Any home cook knows the secret to a perfect cherry pie: almond extract. So why not serve it in a drink? You may want to offer this thick drink with spoons—and as many graham crackers as you want.

½ CUP DRAINED CANNED SOUR CHERRIES
¼ CUP WHITE GRAPE JUICE
2 TABLESPOONS FRESH LIME JUICE
1 TABLESPOON NONALCOHOLIC GRENADINE SYRUP
2 TEASPOONS SUPERFINE SUGAR
1 TEASPOON ALMOND EXTRACT
2 CUPS ICE
2 GRAHAM CRACKERS, FOR GARNISH (OPTIONAL)

Put the sour cherries, white grape juice, lime juice, grenadine syrup, superfine sugar, almond extract, and ice in a blender. Blend until the mixture is uniform and completely smooth.

Pour into two glasses. Garnish each glass with a graham cracker, if desired.

■ Makes two 8-ounce drinks

Cocktail Versions

Before blending, add 2 ounces gold rum to the blender. For an even zippier libation, add 2 ounces spiced rum as well. Or simply add ¼ cup spiced rum. Also, add 2 extra ice cubes to keep the drink thick.

STRAWBERRY MARGARITA SUPREME

If you've been to Mexico in the summer, you know why drinks like these were invented. With or without the addition of ¼ cup tequila, this classic margarita can take the heat out of any scorcher.

8 LARGE SWEET STRAWBERRIES
2 CUPS ICE
⅔ CUP BOTTLED SOUR MIXER OR MARGARITA MIXER
1 TABLESPOON ORANGE JUICE CONCENTRATE, THAWED
2 TEASPOONS BOTTLED SWEETENED LIME JUICE
FRESH STRAWBERRIES, FOR GARNISH (OPTIONAL)

Wash and hull the berries and cut them in half. Then put the berries in a blender with the ice, sour mixer, orange juice concentrate, and sweetened lime juice. Blend until smooth and slushy.

Pour into two glasses and garnish with fresh strawberries, if desired.

■ Makes two 12-ounce drinks

Cocktail Version

Add ¼ cup tequila. Replace the orange juice concentrate with 2 tablespoons Grand Marnier, triple sec, or peach schnapps. Also, add an extra ice cube or two to keep the drink thick and slushy.

Variations

RASPBERRY MARGARITA
Use 15 raspberries instead of the strawberries. Garnish with whole raspberries.

PEACH MARGARITA
Use 2 small unpeeled peaches, sliced and pitted, instead of the strawberries. Garnish with unpeeled fresh peach slices.

CLASSIC PIÑA COLADA

The original piña colada is said to have been invented in Puerto Rico, right after the invention of the blender. Although most recipes call for pineapple juice, try this one with crushed fruit for a drink with more body and texture.

1 (8-OUNCE) CAN CRUSHED PINEAPPLE IN
    UNSWEETENED JUICE (ABOUT 1 HEAPING CUP)
3 CUPS ICE
½ CUP CREAM OF COCONUT (SEE NOTE)

Combine the pineapple, with its juice, the ice, and the cream of coconut in a blender and blend until completely smooth.

Pour into two glasses.

■ Makes two 16-ounce drinks

NOTE: This recipe calls for cream of coconut, which is sweetened, and should not be confused with unsweetened coconut milk, also known as coconut cream.

Cocktail Version

Add ½ cup white or golden rum before blending. Also, add an extra ice cube or two to keep the drink thick and slushy.

Variation

ORANGE PIÑA COLADA
Drain the crushed pineapple and replace the liquid with an equal amount of fresh orange juice.

BANANA COLADA

Bananas blend well with almost any fruit, but they might be at their very best with coconuts. Just remember to use the ripest bananas you can find—darker on the outside means sweeter on the inside.

2 TABLESPOONS SHREDDED COCONUT,
    FOR GARNISH (OPTIONAL)
1 LARGE RIPE BANANA
2 CUPS ICE
¼ CUP CREAM OF COCONUT (SEE NOTE, PAGE 52)
½ CUP WHITE GRAPE JUICE
¼ TEASPOON VANILLA EXTRACT

If using the shredded coconut, preheat the oven to 350 degrees, spread the coconut on a baking sheet, and toast it until lightly brown, about 2–3 minutes, being careful not to burn it. Let cool and set aside.

Peel the banana, break it into pieces, and put them in a blender. Add the ice, cream of coconut, grape juice, and vanilla to the blender. Blend until smooth.

Pour into two tall glasses and top each glass with a tablespoon of toasted coconut, if desired.

■ Makes two 10-ounce drinks

Cocktail Versions

Add 3 ounces white rum (or 1½ ounces white rum and 1½ ounces spiced rum) and 1 ounce banana liqueur. Also, add an extra ice cube or two.

MANDARIN PEACHY COLADA

This drink is delicate in flavor and color. When it is made with juicy, ripe fresh peaches, it is sweet and subtle.

> 1 LARGE RIPE PEACH, RINSED
> ¼ CUP DRAINED CANNED MANDARIN ORANGE SECTIONS
> 2 CUPS ICE
> ¼ CUP CANNED UNSWEETENED COCONUT MILK
>   (SEE NOTE)
> 2 TABLESPOONS ORANGE JUICE CONCENTRATE,
>   THAWED
> FRESH PEACH SLICES, UNPEELED, AND MINT
>   SPRIGS, FOR GARNISH (OPTIONAL)

Rinse and slice the peach, leaving the peel on. Put the peach slices and orange sections in a blender, then add the ice, coconut milk, and orange juice concentrate. Blend until smooth and creamy.

Pour into two glasses and garnish with fresh peach slices and mint sprigs, if desired.

■ Makes two 10-ounce drinks

NOTE: You should be able to find canned unsweetened coconut milk in the Asian food section in almost any supermarket. If not, you can make your own by simmering 8 ounces unsweetened shredded coconut with

Cocktail Version

Add 3 ounces white rum and 1 ounce peach schnapps before blending. Golden rum is delicious but can overpower the peach flavor—use it only if your peaches are exceptionally sweet and juicy. Also, add an extra ice cube or two to keep the drink thick and slushy.

2½ cups water for 10 minutes. Let the mixture cool, then press through a sieve and discard the coconut solids. The remaining liquid will keep, tightly sealed and refrigerated, for up to one month and can be used in place of canned unsweetened coconut milk.

COCOLADA

This frozen treat—chocolate milk, island-style—is fast, simple, and unbelievably light and refreshing. You should be able to find canned unsweetened coconut milk in almost any supermarket, or make your own (see Note, page 54).

> 2 CUPS ICE
> ½ CUP CANNED UNSWEETENED COCONUT MILK
>   (SEE NOTE, PAGE 54)
> ¼ CUP CHOCOLATE SYRUP

Combine the ice, coconut milk, and chocolate syrup in a blender. Blend just until the texture is still icy, not yet slushy.

Pour into a glass.

■ Makes one 16-ounce drink

Cocktail Version

Add 2 ounces Malibu coconut rum and ½ ounce dark crème de cacao. Also, add an extra ice cube or two to keep the drink thick and slushy.

WAIKIKI DAIQUIRI

Pineapples and papayas offer the true taste of Hawaii. For this drink, use only ripe pineapples, ones that have turned a pale yellow and smell very sweet even before you cut into them. If you can't find a ripe pineapple, use canned pineapple chunks instead, draining them thoroughly.

^{2}/$_3$ CUP DRAINED CHOPPED FRESH OR CANNED PINEAPPLE
^{1}/$_4$ CUP PAPAYA NECTAR
2 TABLESPOONS FRESH LIME JUICE
2 TABLESPOONS PASSION FRUIT SYRUP (SEE NOTE)
2 TEASPOONS SUPERFINE SUGAR
1^1/$_2$ CUPS ICE
2 SMALL WEDGES PINEAPPLE, FOR GARNISH (OPTIONAL)

Put the pineapple, papaya nectar, lime juice, passion fruit syrup, superfine sugar, and ice in a blender. Blend until smooth and slushy.

Pour into two glasses. Garnish with pineapple wedges, if desired.

■ Makes two 8-ounce drinks

NOTE: Passion fruit syrup is available in many gourmet and specialty markets. It's a reduced, thickened syrup, not to be confused with passion fruit nectar.

Cocktail Version

Add 3 ounces gold rum before blending, plus 2 additional ice cubes to keep the drink thick and slushy.

LATE SUMMER DAIQUIRI

I love to make this drink at the end of summer when muskmelons and cantaloupes are overflowing at the market and the prices go way down. Only the juiciest, most intensely flavored melons will do. I choose melons that give slightly when pressed, feel heavy in my hands, and have a sweet, musky aroma when I put them right up to my nose. Remember, melons are like pineapples: If they don't smell sweet, they probably don't taste sweet.

> 1/2 SMALL MUSKMELON OR CANTALOUPE
> 1 CUP ICE
> 2 TABLESPOONS HONEY
> 1/8 TEASPOON CINNAMON
> JUICE OF 1 SMALL LIME (ABOUT 1 1/2 TO 2 TABLESPOONS)

Scoop the seeds out of the melon. Cut away the rind and roughly chop the fruit. You will need 1 heaping cup. Combine the melon, ice, honey, cinnamon, and lime juice in a blender and blend until completely smooth.

Pour into two glasses.

■ Makes two 8-ounce drinks

Cocktail Version

Add 2 ounces of white rum before blending. Also add an extra ice cube or two to keep the drink thick and slushy. Or add only 1 1/2 ounces of white rum and 1 ounce of melon liqueur. Don't forget the extra ice to help keep the drink slushy.

Variations

Use pure maple syrup instead of honey.

Substitute ground ginger for the cinnamon.

4 CHOC

AND

COFFEE

CONC

FROZEN HOT CHOCOLATE

Don't give up your favorite hot cocoa just because the temperature is high enough to fry an egg on the sidewalk. This frozen blend of milk chocolate and dark chocolate is just as comforting in July as its hot cousin is in December. Check out all the variations.

1 CUP ICE
½ CUP ICE WATER
2 (1-OUNCE) PACKAGES INSTANT COCOA MIX
(WITHOUT MARSHMALLOWS)
3 TABLESPOONS SEMISWEET CHOCOLATE CHIPS
1 TABLESPOON WHIPPED CREAM

Combine the ice, ice water, and cocoa mixes and 2 tablespoons of the chocolate chips in a blender. Pulse the blender until the mixer starts to blend smoothly. Then switch to high and blend until the chocolate chips are finely ground and the mixture is completely smooth.

Variations
FROZEN RASPBERRY HOT CHOCOLATE Add 1 tablespoon frozen raspberries in syrup (thawed) or 1 tablespoon raspberry jam.
FROZEN NUTTY HOT CHOCOLATE Add 2 tablespoons almond or hazelnut syrup (see page 12).
FROZEN MINT HOT CHOCOLATE Add 2 tablespoons mint syrup (see page 12).
FROZEN SPICED HOT CHOCOLATE Add a pinch of cinnamon or nutmeg.
FROZEN ORANGE HOT CHOCOLATE Add ¼ teaspoon grated orange zest.

Pour into a glass, top with 1 tablespoon whipped cream, and sprinkle with the remaining tablespoon of chocolate chips.

■ **Makes one 12-ounce drink**

CHOCOLATE MINT PARFAIT

If only some kind hotel housekeeper would leave one of these on my pillow instead of a gold-wrapped chocolate mint!

1 CUP ICE
¾ CUP MILK
½ CUP CHOCOLATE ICE CREAM, SOFTENED
3 TABLESPOONS CHOCOLATE SYRUP
⅛ TEASPOON PEPPERMINT EXTRACT (OPTIONAL)
2 (1.5-OUNCE) CHOCOLATE MINT PATTIES

Put the ice, milk, ice cream, chocolate syrup, and peppermint extract, if using, in a blender. Break up one peppermint patty and add it on top. Blend until the mixture is smooth and creamy.

Pour into two glasses and garnish with the remaining peppermint patty, crumbled or whole.

■ **Makes two 10-ounce drinks**

Cocktail Version

Add 1 ounce each dark crème de cacao, white crème de menthe (or peppermint schnapps), and brandy. Reduce milk to ½ cup and add an extra ice cube.

ICED GERMAN CHOCOLATE CAKE

Another variation on a delicious dessert, just as sweet and rich as the original. You can use store-bought brownies or, better yet, bake your own. If you have chocolate fudge cookies on hand, use them instead.

10 SMALL CARAMEL CANDIES
1/4 CUP HEAVY CREAM
1/3 CUP SWEETENED SHREDDED COCONUT
3/4 CUP CHOCOLATE ICE CREAM, MELTED
1/2 CUP CRUMBLED BROWNIES (ABOUT A
    4-INCH SQUARE)
2 CUPS ICE
CHOCOLATE COOKIES AND WHIPPED CREAM,
    FOR GARNISH (OPTIONAL)

Combine the caramels and cream in a small saucepan and place over low heat until the cream starts to bubble and the caramels begin to melt (see Note). Continue to simmer, stirring constantly, until the caramels are completely melted, about 1 minute. Add the coconut and let the mixture simmer for 1 more minute, stirring constantly.

Pour the hot mixture into a blender and blend on high for about 30 seconds, until the coconut is pureed. Allow the mixture to cool slightly, then add the melted ice cream, the crumbled brownies, and the ice. Pulse the blender, if necessary, to get the mixture blending smoothly, then blend on high for about 30 seconds, until smooth and frothy.

Pour into two glasses and garnish with chocolate cookies and whipped cream, if desired.

■ Makes two 12-ounce drinks

NOTE: You can melt the caramel-cream mixture in the microwave: Put the cream and caramels in a deep glass bowl and microwave on high for 2 to 3 minutes, stirring every 30 seconds. Add the coconut after 1 minute and blend. Continue heating.

CHOCOLATE CHERRY BLAST

This drink reminds some people of black forest cake: rich, dense chocolate, dripping with sour cherry filling and whipped cream. Others say it tastes like chocolate-covered cherries gently folded into soft vanilla ice cream. Mix up a batch and decide for yourself.

1/2 CUP ICE
1/2 CUP VANILLA ICE CREAM, SOFTENED
2 TABLESPOONS CHOCOLATE SYRUP
1/2 CUP CANNED PITTED SOUR CHERRIES,
    DRAINED, SYRUP RESERVED
WHIPPED CREAM AND MARASCHINO
    CHERRIES, FOR GARNISH (OPTIONAL)

Combine the ice, ice cream, chocolate syrup, and cherries and 3 tablespoons of the reserved cherry syrup in a blender. Blend until the mixture is thick and smooth.

Pour into a glass and garnish with whipped cream and a maraschino cherry, if desired.

■ Makes one 12-ounce drink

SHIVERING CHOCOLATE MONKEY

This drink is a tribute to all my fellow banana lovers. The recipe calls for banana chips and the ripest banana you can get your opposable thumbs on.

½ CUP CHOCOLATE ICE CREAM, SOFTENED
1 TABLESPOON CREAM OF COCONUT
   (SEE NOTE, PAGE 52)
1 SMALL RIPE BANANA, PEELED
1 CUP ICE
½ CUP HALF-AND-HALF
2 TABLESPOONS CHOCOLATE SYRUP
½ CUP SWEETENED BANANA CHIPS,
   ABOUT 20 TO 25 CHIPS (SEE NOTE)
DIAGONAL SLICES OF BANANA, DIPPED IN CHOCOLATE
   SYRUP AND COCONUT FLAKES,
   FOR GARNISH (OPTIONAL)

Put the ice cream and the cream of coconut in a blender. Break the banana into 3 or 4 pieces, and add it to the blender with the ice, half-and-half, and chocolate syrup. Blend until smooth and creamy. Turn off the blender and add the banana chips. Blend on high until the chips are completely crushed and incorporated (about 15 to 20 seconds).

Pour into two glasses and garnish with the coated banana slices, if desired.

■ Makes two 10-ounce drinks

NOTE: Banana chips come sweetened and unsweetened, and both are available at most supermarkets or natural food stores. Use the sweetened kind for the best flavor. Don't be fooled by plantain chips, which look like banana chips but taste more like potatoes than bananas.

HAZELNUT COFFEE FRAPPÉ

This thick shake, like the best hazelnut-flavored coffee at a gourmet store, is guaranteed to calm your sweet tooth—that is, until you've reached the bottom of the glass.

1 ROUNDED TEASPOON INSTANT ESPRESSO POWDER
(OR INSTANT COFFEE)
2 TABLESPOONS HOT WATER
1 CUP VANILLA ICE CREAM
¼ CUP MILK
2 TABLESPOONS HAZELNUT SYRUP
1 CUP ICE
2 TABLESPOONS GROUND HAZELNUTS, FOR GARNISH
(OPTIONAL)

In a small bowl, combine the instant espresso powder and water. Stir until dissolved. Place this mixture in a blender. Add the vanilla ice cream, milk, hazelnut syrup, and ice. Blend until smooth and silky.

Pour into two glasses. Garnish with ground hazelnuts, sprinkled over the top of the drinks, if desired.

■ Makes two 8-ounce drinks

Cocktail Versions

For a rich treat, add 2 ounces coffee liqueur before blending. If you want to make a frozen coffee brandy alexander, add 2 ounces chocolate liqueur as well. Add 2 or 3 additional ice cubes to keep the drink thick.

FROZEN PEANUT BUTTER CHOCOLATE MALTED

The intensity of the peanut butter in this recipe is balanced by low-fat or nonfat chocolate ice cream and skim milk. But if you're in the mood to truly indulge yourself, use whole milk and the richest ice cream you can find.

1 CUP LOW-FAT OR NONFAT CHOCOLATE
   ICE CREAM, SOFTENED
2 TABLESPOONS CREAMY PEANUT BUTTER
¼ CUP CHOCOLATE SYRUP
1 CUP ICE
¾ CUP SKIM MILK
1 HEAPING TABLESPOON PLAIN MALTED
   MILK POWDER (SEE NOTE)
2 SMALL PEANUT-BUTTER CUP CANDIES,
   FOR GARNISH (OPTIONAL)

Combine the ice cream, peanut butter, chocolate syrup, ice, milk, and malted milk powder in a blender. Pulse the blender until the mixture blends easily. Blend until smooth.

Pour into two tall glasses and crumble the peanut-butter cups on top, if desired.

■ Makes two 10-ounce drinks

NOTE: Malted milk powder is available at many supermarkets and health food stores.

QUADRUPLE COFFEE SHAKE

If lying around in the sun tires you out, here is the perfect source of rejuvenation.

> 2 CUPS FRESH BREWED COFFEE, COOLED
> 2 TEASPOONS INSTANT ESPRESSO
> 1 CUP COFFEE ICE CREAM, MELTED
> 1 TABLESPOON COFFEE SYRUP (SEE PAGE 12)

Pour the brewed coffee into ice cube trays, filling them only halfway. Freeze the trays. Put 1½ cups of the coffee ice cubes in a blender along with the instant espresso, melted ice cream, and coffee syrup. Blend until smooth.

Pour into two glasses.

■ **Makes two 8-ounce drinks**

Variations
CAPPUCCINO COFFEE SHAKE Add a pinch of cinnamon.
FLAVORED COFFEE SHAKE Use flavored coffee—such as vanilla, Irish cream, or hazelnut—to make the ice cubes.

COFFEEHOUSE FRAPPUCCINO

This takes seconds to make if you keep a batch of Coffee Master Mix (see page 69) in the refrigerator. Simply blend it with ice whenever you like and add whatever flavors you are in the mood for when you blend it all together (see Variations below).

1 CUP ICE
$1/2$ CUP COFFEE MASTER MIX (RECIPE FOLLOWS)
GROUND CINNAMON
CHOCOLATE-COVERED COFFEE BEANS, FOR GARNISH
(OPTIONAL)

Put the ice into a blender. Pour in the Coffee Master Mix. Pulse the blender until the mixture is thick and frosty.

Pour into a glass, top with ground cinnamon, and garnish with a few chocolate-covered coffee beans, if desired.

■ Makes one 10-ounce drink

Cocktail Version

Try 2 tablespoons coffee, mint, Irish cream, or chocolate-flavored liqueur. Just add the liqueur before blending, and don't forget to add an extra ice cube or two.

Variations

Add 2 tablespoons any flavored syrup you like before blending. Hazelnut, almond, and chocolate are especially good. When adding syrup, also add 1 or 2 extra ice cubes or the drink may be too sweet (see page 15).

COFFEE MASTER MIX

1 CUP STRONG BREWED ESPRESSO
1 CUP DARK CORN SYRUP
1/2 CUP VERY FRESH LOW-FAT MILK
1/4 CUP NONFAT DRY MILK
1/4 TEASPOON VANILLA EXTRACT

Combine the espresso, corn syrup, fresh milk, dry milk, and vanilla in a large jar or pitcher. Stir or shake until the corn syrup and dry milk are completely dissolved. Cover and refrigerate until needed. Shake the mixture well before each use. This should keep for about a week (see Note).

■ Makes 2 1/2 cups

NOTE: The fresher your milk is, the longer the Coffee Master Mix will last in the refrigerator.

TRIPLE CHOCOLATE MALT

Who doesn't like chocolate ice cream, chocolate sorbet, and chocolate syrup? And who wouldn't like them all together? There's no better way to satisfy your chocolate cravings than a tall glass of this malt, either on a lazy afternoon or late at night, when your favorite old movie is on TV.

1 CUP CHOCOLATE ICE CREAM
1 CUP CHOCOLATE SORBET
1 CUP MILK
¼ CUP CHOCOLATE SYRUP
⅓ CUP PLAIN MALTED MILK POWDER
6 MALTED MILK BALLS, FOR GARNISH (OPTIONAL)

Put the chocolate ice cream, chocolate sorbet, milk, chocolate syrup, and malted milk powder in a blender. Pulse several times to get the mixture combined, then blend until the malt is smooth, about 30 seconds.

Pour into two glasses. Garnish with malted milk balls, if desired.

■ Makes two 16-ounce drinks

Cocktail Versions

Omit the chocolate syrup. Add ¼ cup chocolate liqueur and ¼ cup vodka before blending. Add an extra ½ cup ice cream or sorbet to keep the drink thick. For a different take on this thick malt, you can omit the chocolate liqueur and add ¼ cup coffee liqueur or hazelnut liqueur before blending.

Variation

If you're watching your diet, you can use nonfat ice cream and skim milk.

CARAMEL WALNUT CAPPUCCINO COFFEE CAKE SHAKE

This frozen drink combines the best of breakfast in a glass, so don't be afraid to start your day with one.

2 CUPS EXTRA-STRONG COFFEE,
   COOLED (SEE NOTE)
2 TABLESPOONS CARAMEL ICE CREAM TOPPING
2 TABLESPOONS WET WALNUT ICE CREAM TOPPING
½ CUP HALF-AND-HALF
PINCH OF GROUND CINNAMON

Pour the cooled coffee into ice cube trays, filling them halfway, and freeze.

Combine the frozen cubes, caramel topping, walnut topping, half-and-half, and cinnamon in a blender. Blend until the nuts are completely pulverized. You may need to pulse the blender to completely blend this drink.

■ Makes about two 12-ounce drinks

NOTE: To make extra-strong coffee, use 1½ times the amount of ground or instant coffee you normally use.

5 ICE
AND
OTHER
RICH
IND

CREAM

ULGENCES

ORANGE VANILLA SWIRL

Somebody once dipped rich vanilla ice cream into a sunny-sweet orange ice to invent the Creamsicle, and summer has never been the same since. Now you can enjoy this classic flavor combination swirled together in a tall frosted glass instead of on a Popsicle stick. To frost a glass, simply place it in the freezer for 10 minutes before you are ready to use it.

ORANGE MIXTURE
½ CUP FRESH ORANGE JUICE
¼ CUP ORANGE SHERBET
VANILLA MIXTURE
⅓ CUP MILK
¼ CUP VANILLA ICE CREAM
1 TABLESPOON VANILLA SYRUP (SEE PAGE 12)

Blend the orange juice and orange sherbet in a blender until smooth. If you have a second blender container, blend the vanilla mixture and then combine it with the orange mixture in the glass. Otherwise pour this orange slush into a freezerproof container and keep it in the freezer while you rinse your blender container and repeat the process with the milk, vanilla ice cream, and vanilla syrup. Alternatively, pour each mixture into a frosted tall ice cream soda glass. The mixtures will intermingle, creating a swirl pattern.

■ Makes one 16-ounce drink

Cocktail Version

Add 1 ounce Grand Marnier or triple sec to the orange mixture. Replace the vanilla syrup with Cure 43 or Tuaca, two vanilla-flavored liqueurs. Or use amaretto for a unique twist on an old favorite.

74

BANANA CARAMEL DELIGHT

Caramel syrup is a thickened, burnt-sugar syrup, available in many gourmet markets and in Italian specialty stores. In this drink, the syrup gets blended with banana and almonds for a decadent creamy treat you won't soon forget. It's like bananas foster in a glass. And the ice is a surprising but common ingredient in many malts and shakes—it gives lots of body to the drink.

1 RIPE BANANA
1 CUP VANILLA ICE CREAM
2 TABLESPOONS CARAMEL SYRUP OR 2 TABLESPOONS
   CARAMEL TOPPING
½ CUP MILK
1 CUP ICE
4 CARAMEL CANDIES, FOR GARNISH (OPTIONAL)

Peel the banana and cut it into quarters. Put them in the blender. Add the vanilla ice cream, caramel syrup, milk, and ice. Blend until the drink is smooth.

Pour into two glasses. Garnish each glass with two caramel candies, if desired.

■ Makes two 10-ounce drinks

Cocktail Version

Add ¼ cup vodka and 2 ounces banana liqueur to the blender, as well as another 1 or 2 additional ice cubes to keep the drink thick.

75

ESKIMO ALMOND FROST

With chocolate syrup on the top and the bottom of each drink, this concoction looks like a classic ice cream sandwich in a glass. But the "filling" is even better: made from vanilla ice cream and toasted almonds. It's a unique and satisfying twist.

2 TABLESPOONS SLICED ALMONDS
1 CUP VANILLA ICE CREAM
2 TABLESPOONS ALMOND SYRUP (ALSO CALLED "ORGEAT," OR "ORZATA"; SEE NOTE, PAGE 26)
½ CUP MILK
½ CUP ICE
¼ CUP CHOCOLATE SYRUP, DIVIDED

In a small skillet over medium heat, toast the sliced almonds for 3 minutes, shaking the pan occasionally to keep them from burning. Cool the almonds on a separate plate for 5 minutes.

Put the toasted almonds, vanilla ice cream, almond syrup, milk, and ice in a blender. Blend until the drink is smooth.

Place 1 tablespoon chocolate syrup in the bottom of each of two glasses. Divide the ice cream mixture between them. Top each with another tablespoon of chocolate syrup. Serve with a straw.

■ Makes two 8-ounce drinks

Cocktail Versions

For a light cocktail, add 3 ounces amaretto before blending the ice cream mixture. For a more potent version, add 3 tablespoons vodka as well. In either case, add an additional 1 or 2 ice cubes to keep the drink thick.

FROZEN KEY LIME PIE

This drink is just as refreshing as its namesake dessert. Reduced-fat or fat-free sweetened condensed milk might take the edge off the guilt, but for total indulgence, go for the real thing and use heavy cream.

1½ CUPS ICE
½ CUP SWEETENED CONDENSED MILK
⅓ CUP KEY LIME JUICE (SEE NOTE)
¼ CUP ICE WATER
8 GINGERSNAPS
2 TABLESPOONS WHIPPED CREAM

Put the ice in a blender. Add the sweetened condensed milk, lime juice, and ice water. Crumble 4 gingersnaps on top. Pulse the blender until the mixture blends easily. Blend until completely smooth.

Serve in small glasses and top each drink with a dollop of whipped cream and 2 of the remaining gingersnaps.

■ Makes two 8-ounce drinks

NOTE: Bottled key lime juice is available in most supermarkets. If you can't find it, lemon juice can be used, giving your drink the subtle flavor of old-fashioned lemon meringue pie.

Cocktail Versions

Add 2 ounces white rum before blending. Also, add an extra ice cube or two to keep the drink thick and slushy.

If you choose to use lemon juice, 2 ounces vodka or lemon-flavored vodka works even better than rum. Don't forget the extra ice.

APPLE COBBLER SMOOTHIE

What's the only thing better than eating fresh apple pie? Being able to drink it, of course! This apple smoothie is thick, sweet, and wonderful. It makes a perfect dessert—if you can wait that long.

¼ CUP PECANS
1 ½ CUPS VANILLA ICE CREAM
1 CUP CANNED APPLE PIE FILLING
½ CUP MILK
¼ TEASPOON GROUND CINNAMON
1 CUP ICE
2 TABLESPOONS RAISINS, FOR GARNISH (OPTIONAL)

In a small skillet set over medium heat, toast the pecans until they are lightly browned and give off a nutty smell, about 3 minutes. Shake the pan occasionally to keep the nuts from burning. Cool them on a separate plate for 5 minutes.

Put the toasted pecans, vanilla ice cream, apple pie filling, milk, cinnamon, and ice in a blender. Pulse three or four times to combine the drink, scraping down the sides between pulses if necessary. Blend the drink until smooth.

Pour into two glasses. Garnish with raisins sprinkled over the top, if desired.

■ Makes two 12-ounce drinks

Cocktail Versions

Add ¼ cup vodka before blending. For a deeper taste, add ¼ cup brandy instead. Or you can add ¼ cup apple schnapps. In any event, add 2 or 3 additional ice cubes, to keep the drink thick.

EGGNOG TOBOGGAN

Most people love eggnog but never think to indulge in it except during the holidays. This recipe is fast and easy with prepared eggnog. The canned variety is available year-round in most supermarkets and is safer than homemade, which contains raw eggs.

> 1 CUP PREPARED EGGNOG
> 1½ CUPS ICE
> 1 TEASPOON IMITATION RUM FLAVORING
> 2 TABLESPOONS APRICOT JAM
> ⅛ TEASPOON GROUND CINNAMON (OPTIONAL)
> PINCH OF GRATED NUTMEG

Pour the eggnog into a blender. Add the ice, rum flavoring, apricot jam, and cinnamon, if using. Pulse the blender until the mixture blends smoothly. Then blend on high for 30 seconds, or until completely smooth.

Pour into two glasses and top with grated nutmeg.

■ Makes two 10-ounce drinks

Variation

BANANA EGGNOG TOBOGGAN
For an even creamier, richer-flavored eggnog, add one small very ripe banana before blending.

Cocktail Version

Add 3 ounces dark rum before blending and omit the rum flavoring. Also, add an extra ice cube or two to keep the drink thick and slushy.

S'MORES SMOOTHIE

This combination of chocolate, marshmallows, and graham crackers has become a classic for kids and adults. Today, you can enjoy the taste of s'mores by the campfire, from the barbecue or the toaster oven, even in a breakfast cereal! Using marshmallow creme instead of marshmallows makes it a snap to blend up this frozen-drink version of the classic treat.

1/2 CUP MARSHMALLOW CREME
1/4 CUP CHOCOLATE SYRUP
1 CUP MILK
2 CUPS ICE
2 GRAHAM CRACKER SQUARES,
    PLUS EXTRA FOR SERVING
MINI MARSHMALLOWS AND CHOCOLATE
    CHIPS, FOR GARNISH (OPTIONAL)

Put the marshmallow creme in a blender. Pour in the chocolate syrup and milk. Put the ice on top and crumble the graham crackers over the top. Cover the blender and pulse until the mixture blends smoothly, then blend on high for at least 30 seconds, or until the marshmallow creme has been completely incorporated.

Pour into two glasses and garnish with mini marshmallows and chocolate chips, if desired. Serve with extra graham crackers.

■ Makes two 10-ounce drinks

PUMPKIN FROST

While this drink is perfect for a holiday dessert, you won't want to serve it only in late November. You can have the homey taste of autumn all year round, especially when the heat of summer makes you think those clear, crisp days may never come.

1½ CUPS VANILLA ICE CREAM
¾ CUP CANNED PUMPKIN
¼ CUP PLUS 2 TABLESPOONS MAPLE SYRUP
¾ CUP ICE
¼ TEASPOON GROUND CINNAMON
⅛ TEASPOON GROUND CLOVES
⅛ TEASPOON GRATED NUTMEG
2 GINGER SNAPS, FOR GARNISH (OPTIONAL)

Put the vanilla ice cream, pumpkin, maple syrup, ice, cinnamon, cloves, and nutmeg in a blender. Pulse three or four times to get the drink blended, then blend at high speed until well combined.

Pour into two glasses. Garnish with ginger snaps, if desired.

■ Makes two 10-ounce drinks

Variations

You can add ½ cup drained canned (not fresh) pineapple before blending, for a more tropical taste. Or use ½ cup drained canned mandarin oranges before blending, for a Pumpkin Orange Frost. You can even blend 4 ginger snaps into the drink itself for a thicker, more luscious libation.

BLUEBERRIES, PEACHES, AND CREAM

If you are lucky enough to have wild blueberries growing near your house, pick as many as you can, mix up a batch of frozen drinks, and freeze the remaining berries. Blueberries freeze quite well and retain their flavor and sweetness. But like most berries, they can be limp and soggy when defrosted, so measure them while they are still frozen, then use them after they've thawed out.

½ CUP BLUEBERRIES, STEMS REMOVED
½ CUP PEACH NECTAR
1½ CUPS ICE
1 CUP VANILLA ICE CREAM, SOFTENED
⅛ TEASPOON ALMOND EXTRACT
¼ TEASPOON GROUND CINNAMON (OPTIONAL)
FRESH UNPEELED PEACH SLICES, FOR GARNISH (OPTIONAL)

Variations

RASPBERRIES OR BLACKBERRIES, PEACHES, AND CREAM
Use raspberries or blackberries instead of blueberries.

BLUEBERRIES, APRICOTS, AND CREAM
Using apricot nectar instead of peach nectar gives a slightly more tangy taste to the drink.

Variations

NUTTY BLUEBERRIES, PEACHES, AND CREAM
The addition of ¼ cup hazelnuts or almonds before blending gives the drink incredible texture and flavor.

FRESH FRUIT COBBLER SMOOTHIE
Blend in one graham cracker square or a few crumbled gingersnaps for the flavor of a fresh fruit cobbler.

BLUEBERRIES, PEACHES, AND YOGURT
Nonfat or low-fat vanilla yogurt instead of ice cream tastes great and cuts the fat content significantly.

Put the blueberries, peach nectar, ice, vanilla ice cream, almond extract, and cinnamon, if using, in a blender. Pulse the blender until the mixture blends smoothly, then blend on high for 10 seconds.

Pour into two glasses and garnish with peach slices, if using.

■ **Makes two 12-ounce drinks**

BUTTERSCOTCH WHIRL

Butterscotch lovers beware: This recipe may push you over the top.

> 1/2 CUP BUTTER PECAN ICE CREAM, SOFTENED
> 1/2 CUP MILK
> 1 CUP ICE
> 2 TABLESPOONS BUTTERSCOTCH TOPPING
> 1 BUTTERFINGER CANDY BAR
> 2 TABLESPOONS WHIPPED CREAM
> 2 TABLESPOONS BUTTERSCOTCH CHIPS (OPTIONAL)

Combine the ice cream, milk, ice, and butterscotch topping in a blender. Crumble 1/2 the candy bar on top. Blend the mixture until the ice is crushed and the nuts and candy bar are completely smooth.

Pour into two tall glasses, top each with 1 tablespoon of whipped cream, and garnish each with 1 tablespoon of butterscotch chips, if desired.

■ **Makes two 10-ounce drinks**

Cocktail Version

Replace butterscotch topping with 3 ounces butterscotch schnapps. Also, add an extra ice cube or two to keep the drink thick and slushy.

6 GRA

SORB

NITAS AND ETS

Although technically not drinks, the icy and refreshing desserts called granitas and sorbets have earned their place among these incredible frozen coolers.

GAZPACHO GRANITA

Not all granitas are sweet. Consider this spicy icicle: Cool and light, it delivers an unexpected kick of peppers, tomato, and vinegar and makes a great first course for an outdoor dinner party or a refreshing afternoon snack. But plan ahead, because the mixture should sit overnight in the refrigerator to mellow before freezing.

3 CUPS TOMATO JUICE
2 GREEN PEPPERS, CORED, SEEDED,
   AND DICED
1/4 CUP MINCED ONION
1 CLOVE GARLIC, CHOPPED
2 TABLESPOONS RED WINE VINEGAR
2 TABLESPOONS FRESH LEMON JUICE
2 TEASPOONS WORCESTERSHIRE SAUCE
1 TEASPOON SALT
1/2 TEASPOON WHOLE CELERY SEED
1/4 TEASPOON GROUND BLACK PEPPER
5 OR 6 SHAKES OF TABASCO
SALT AND PEPPER TO TASTE (OPTIONAL)
ITALIAN PARSLEY SPRIGS OR CILANTRO
   SPRIGS, FOR GARNISH (OPTIONAL)

Combine the tomato juice, green peppers, onion, garlic, vinegar, lemon juice, Worcestershire sauce, salt, celery seed, black pepper, and Tabasco in a bowl or large pitcher. Cover and refrigerate overnight.

The following day, put a metal bowl in the freezer for at least 1 hour. Puree the mixture in the blender (you may need to do this in batches). Taste for seasoning and add salt and pepper, if necessary.

Strain into the cold metal bowl and put the bowl back in the freezer. Scrape around the edges every half hour until the mixture is thick and slushy. Then cover and freeze until firm.

To serve, scrape out with a flat steel ice cream spade or a heavy-duty ice cream scoop (see Note).

Garnish with the parsley sprigs or cilantro sprigs, if desired.

■ Serves 6 to 8

NOTE: Alternatively, you can freeze the mixture in ice cube trays, filling them halfway. Chop the frozen cubes into soft ices in the blender by pulsing it. Then return the slushy mixture to the freezer until completely firm.

Cocktail Version

A shot of iced vodka poured on top of a frosty dish of gazpacho granita is better than any Bloody Mary you can imagine.

CURRIED CARROT GRANITA

Curry and yogurt blend together to make this a wonderful accompaniment to Indian cuisine. If you have a juicer, make your own carrot juice for this drink. If not, many supermarkets and natural food stores make fresh carrot juice in their produce department. In a pinch, canned carrot juice works just fine. Look for it in the juice section or even in the baby food aisle.

> 2 CUPS CARROT JUICE
> ¼ CUP DARK BROWN SUGAR
> 1 TEASPOON MILD CURRY POWDER
> ¼ CUP PLAIN YOGURT (OPTIONAL)
> CARROT CURLS, FOR GARNISH

Put a metal mixing bowl in the freezer for an hour before you begin. Put the carrot juice, brown sugar, curry powder, and yogurt, if using, in a blender. Blend until the sugar is dissolved and the yogurt is completely incorporated. Remove the bowl from the freezer and strain the mixture into the bowl. Put back in the freezer and scrape around the edges every half hour until the mixture is thick and slushy. Then cover and freeze until firm.

To serve, scrape out with a flat steel ice cream spade or a heavy-duty ice cream scoop (see Note). Garnish with carrot curls.

■ Serves 4 to 6

NOTE: Alternatively, you can freeze the mixture in ice cube trays, filling them halfway. Chop the frozen cubes into soft ices in the blender by pulsing it. Then return the slushy mixture to the freezer until completely firm.

CUCUMBER MINT GRANITA

This delicately flavored ice is especially cooling on a hot afternoon, whether you've been working out, mowing the lawn, or just swinging in the hammock.

1 LARGE CUCUMBER
½ CUP ICE
2 TABLESPOONS HONEY
1 TABLESPOON FRESH LEMON JUICE
2–3 MINT LEAVES
FRESH MINT SPRIGS, FOR GARNISH (OPTIONAL)

Put a metal mixing bowl in the freezer for an hour before you begin. Peel the cucumber, slice it in half lengthwise, and scoop out the seeds with a spoon. Roughly chop the cucumber and put in a blender with the ice, honey, lemon juice, and mint leaves. Pulse the blender until the mixture is smooth. Remove the bowl from the freezer and pour the mixture into the bowl. Put back in the freezer and scrape around the edges every half hour until the mixture is thick and slushy. Then cover and freeze until firm.

To serve, scrape out with a flat steel ice cream spade or a heavy-duty ice cream scoop (see Note on page 88). Garnish with fresh mint sprigs, if desired.

■ Serves 2

PEAR, GINGER, AND GINSENG SORBET

This combination of creamy poached pears with ginger and ginseng is as refreshing as it is different. Use fresh pears and fresh ginger, if they are available. Ground ginger has a milder taste than the fresh root, and canned pears don't have the intense flavor of fresh ones.

> 2 RIPE PEARS
> 2 CUPS WATER
> ½ CUP SUGAR
> 2 SLICES PEELED FRESH GINGER, ABOUT
>   ½ INCH THICK
> JUICE OF ½ SMALL LEMON
>   (ABOUT 1½ TABLESPOONS)
> 1 (10-ML) VIAL PANAX GINSENG
>   EXTRACT (OPTIONAL) (SEE NOTE)

Peel the pears and cut in half. Cut out the core (a melon baller works well for this) and stem. Set aside.

Put the 2 cups water and the sugar, ginger, and lemon juice in a small saucepan and bring to a boil over high heat, stirring, until the sugar is dissolved. Add the pears. Cover and simmer over low heat for 15 minutes, or until the pears are tender when pierced with the point of a knife. Remove from heat.

Remove the pears from the syrup and put them in a blender. Strain the syrup. Add 1 cup of the syrup to the pears and blend until the mixture is pureed. Let the mixture cool, then mix in the ginseng extract, if using.

If you have an automatic ice cream maker, pour the pear mixture into it and follow the manufacturer's directions. Alternatively, pour the mixture into a cold metal bowl and place in the freezer. Stir with a whisk every half hour to break up the ice crystals.

When the mixture is thick and slushy, cover and let freeze until firm.

To serve, scrape out with a heavy metal ice cream scoop. If the sorbet is too hard to scoop, let it soften at room temperature for 10 to 15 minutes prior to serving.

■ **Serves 6 to 8**

NOTE: Panax ginseng extract is a Chinese herb with a gingerlike bite, and it is fabled to be a cure-all for everything from aging to cancer and diabetes. The extract is available in many forms, including 10-ml vials of liquid, which can be found in most natural food stores and Asian markets. See the resource guide at the back of the book.

APRICOT JALAPEÑO SORBET

Dried apricots come in many colors, sizes, and flavors. Try to find Turkish apricots for this sorbet. They are usually thick and chewy with a high sugar content that offsets the spiciness of the peppers nicely and a bright-orange color that won't darken when cooked.

1 JALAPEÑO
½ CUP SUGAR
2 CUPS WATER
½ CUP TURKISH DRIED APRICOTS (ABOUT 4 OUNCES)

Slice the jalapeño into ¼-inch slices (see Note). Put the jalapeño slices and sugar in a small saucepan with the 2 cups water. Bring to a boil over high heat and simmer, stirring, until the sugar is dissolved. Add the apricots, lower the heat, and simmer uncovered for a half hour.

Remove the apricots from the syrup and put them in a blender. Strain the syrup. Add ⅓ cup of the syrup and 1 cup water to the apricots and blend until the mixture is pureed. Let the mixture cool.

If you have an automatic ice cream maker, pour the apricot mixture into it and follow the manufacturer's directions. Alternatively, pour the mixture into a cold metal bowl and place in the freezer.

Stir with a whisk every half hour to break up the ice crystals. When the mixture is thick and slushy, cover and let freeze until firm.

To serve, scrape out with a heavy metal ice cream scoop. If the sorbet is too hard to scoop, let it soften at room temperature for 10 to 15 minutes before serving.

■ Serves 6 to 8

NOTE: Wear plastic gloves or wash your hands well after handling the sliced hot pepper to avoid irritation.

RESOURCE GUIDE

The following stores carry some or all of the fruit nectars, syrups, coconut milk, ginseng extract, as well as much of the fresh and canned tropical fruits called for in this book. The availability of some products may be limited by season, and the shipping of fresh produce may not always be possible; however, all of these stores take mail-order requests and accept major credit cards, and they'll try their best to provide you with what you need.

BREAD & CIRCUS/WHOLE FOODS
15 Washington Street
Brookline,
Massachusetts 02146
1-(800)-780-3663

In the South, this wonderful store is known as Whole Foods, where they carry many organic products. The Northeast knows them as Bread & Circus. I have rarely seen a wider variety of packaged goods, including syrups, nectars, honeys, and coconut milk, as well as common and exotic produce. All mail orders are handled out of their Brighton, Massachusetts, store, which may limit the availability of some fruits, but they will do what they can to send you what you need.

CENTRAL MARKET
4001 North Lamar
Austin, Texas 78756
1-(800)-360-2552
http://www.centralmar-ket.com/

Central Market has one of the largest selections of fresh produce, both common and exotic, as well as the most extensive array of syrups, nectars, canned fruits, nuts, spices, and flavorings I have ever seen. They are very friendly and will do their best to get you whatever you need. If you are in Austin, you should not miss this incredible store and cooking school.

CHINESE-AMERICAN TRADING CO.
91 Mulberry Street
New York, New York 10013
(212) 267-5224

This store is a great resource for ginseng extracts, coconut milk, and some canned tropical fruits, although minimum purchases may be required for shipping.

DEAN & DELUCA
560 Broadway
New York, New York 10012
(212) 431-1691

This gourmet shop in downtown New York City carries almost every flavor of syrup and nectar called for in this book, as well as an extensive line of fresh produce year-round, including many exotic fruits.

GARDEN OF EDEN
162 West 23rd Street
New York, New York 10011
(212) 675-6300

This new and still-growing store will begin filling mail orders in early spring of 1997. They carry many fruit syrups and nectars, and they have a wide variety of fresh, exotic fruits.

ZABAR'S
2245 Broadway
New York, New York 10024
(212) 787-2000

Zabar's carries a wide range of gourmet food products, including syrups, nectars, spices, and coconut milk. They do not carry fresh produce, but they do offer a wide selection of canned exotic fruits.

INDEX